The Dog Observed

Toby, 1923

Look at my dog Toby: doesn't he appear
to have endless possibilities in store for him?
A whole life in front of him?

— Jacques-Henri Lartigue

The Dog Observed

Photographs, 1844–1988

——Edited by Ruth Silverman——

Chronicle Books • San Francisco

Revised Chronicle Books Edition 1988

Printed in Japan.

Library of Congress Cataloging in Publication Data
Silverman, Ruth.
The dog observed.
1. Dogs–pictorial works–Exhibitions.
2. Photography of dogs–Exhibitions. I. Title.
SF430.S5   1984   779'.32   84-47861
ISBN: 0-87701-499-X

Copyright information for the photographs can be found on page 161.

Copy photography: Scott Hyde
Book design: Judith Henry and Iris Weinstein

Distributed in Canada by
Raincoast Books
112 East Third Avenue
Vancouver, B.C.
V5T 1C8

10 9 8 7 6 5 4 3 2

Chronicle Books
San Francisco, California

For my father

Acknowledgments

To the photographers and lenders of the material in this book, whose support of the project from the beginning so pleased me, I offer my greatest appreciation and thanks; their credits appear on page 161. Special thanks are due Antonio Mendoza, who led me to Victoria Wilson at Knopf. In an office already filled with photographs and dog-curios, she said "yes" without hesitation and became the perfect editor. William Secord, Director of The Dog Museum of America, brought the project into being by agreeing to sponsor the exhibition of *The Dog Observed*, on which this book is based. I am grateful for the opportunity he made available and for all the assistance he provided along the way. My agent, Jonathan Dolger, deserves great credit for his kind and patient guidance of a novice in the world of commercial publishing. In addition, I received the help and encouragement of many others whose enthusiasm made my work thoroughly enjoyable and whose contributions made the book possible. I give my thanks to all those mentioned here.

Gerry Ackerman; Robert Adams; Ahn's Stationery; Andy Anderson, University of Louisville; Alfred Appel; Beverly Brannon, The Library of Congress; Mrs. Manuel Alvarez Bravo; Stephen Brigidi; Dr. Ronald Burk, The Animal Medical Center, New York; William Burke; Cornell Capa, International Center of Photography, New York; Natasha Chassagne and Elizabeth Gallin, Magnum Photos; Izora Cohl; Janis Conner and Joel Rosenkrantz; Bruce Cratsley, Marlborough Gallery, New York; Fearn Cutler; Henri Dauman; Mary Donlon; Shelley Dowell, Avedon Studio; Laney Dunn, The Dog Museum of America, New York; Sally Eauclaire; Diana Edkins, Condé Nast, New York; Owen Edwards; Carol Ehlers, Frumkin Gallery, Chicago; Anne Ehrenkranz; Brooke Elkan; Leah Eskin; Betsy Evans; William A. Ewing, International Center of Photography, New York; Joan Fitzsimmons; Larry Fong, Center for Creative Photography, Tucson; Sharon Frost, New York Public Library; Julie Gallant and Martin Bondell, fotofolio; Edna Ghertler, International Center of Photography, New York; Leslie Goldman; Abby Goldstein;

Barbara Grosset, Rapho, Paris; Anita Grossman, Holly Solomon Gallery, New York; Ellen Grossman; Heather Hamilton; Anne Horton, Sotheby's, New York; Marvin Hoshino; Sharon Howell and Glenn Halverson, Walker Art Center, Minneapolis; Andy Hughes; Scott Hyde; Isabelle Jammes; Jessie and Noodle; Alan Klotz, Photocollect, New York; Cliff and Michele Krainik, Krainik Gallery, Washington, D.C.; Richard Lee; Dennis Longwell; Bernard Marbot, Bibliothèque Nationale, Paris; Marie Martin, Martin Gallery, Washington, D.C.; Grace M. Mayer, The Museum of Modern Art, New York; Cheryl Mayor; Joyce and Robert Menschel; Cindy Miller; Margaretta Mitchell; Grant Nicolson; José Orraca; Joan Pedzich, International Museum of Photography at George Eastman House, Rochester, New York; M. Poulet-Allamagny, Caisse Nationale, Paris; Toby Quitslund; C. Roger, Société Française, Paris; Jack Sal; Kate Schlessinger; Leslie Seldin; Lee Sievan, International Center of Photography, New York; Robin Simonson, The Dog Museum of America, New York; Marthe Smith and Courty Hoyt, Life Picture Service; Robert Sobiesek, International Museum of Photography at George Eastman House, Rochester, New York; Staley/Wise Gallery, New York; Rick Tardiff, Horst Studio; George Thomas and Craig Garcia, The Whatcom Museum, Bellingham, Washington; Richard Tooke, The Museum of Modern Art, New York; Roberta Vesley, The American Kennel Club; Lynne Warren, The Museum of Contemporary Art, Chicago; Joan Weich, The Animal Medical Center, New York; Richard Whelan; Roger B. White; Tiana Wimmer, Daniel Wolf, Inc., New York; Anna Winand, International Center of Photography, New York; Jacqui Wong; Koko Yamagishi.

Introduction

"My first picture was of the neighbour's dog, a friendly little animal who wagged his tail at the moment of exposure
so that the result resembled a fan where there should have
been a tail, which pleased me greatly."
—Alvin Langdon Coburn

The dog has been portrayed in art from the first Paleolithic cave
drawings through all phases of both Eastern and Western art. He is
seen as the dog-god of ancient Egypt, the tiny sleeve-dogs of impe-
rial China, hunting hounds in Renaissance painting, and is frequently shown, as both form and symbol, in contemporary
painting, sculpture, and craft. "From the beginning of the Middle
Ages when the dog was generally allowed to be present in noble
society," writes Fernand Mery, "the more it was loved the more artists began to regard it as an interesting subject."* What we know
about the human-canine bond, one that may reach back 25,000
years or more, and the dog's myriad social roles, from friend to foe,
as servant and sacred object, is in large measure determined by the
depiction of the dog in art.

The study of the dog in art makes a scientific contribution as well,
for it presents much of the evidence we possess of canine forms that

*Fernand Mery, *The Life, History and Magic of the Dog* (New York: Grosset and Dunlap, 1968).

have since become altered by natural or selective breeding and helps trace the mysterious genetic trail that leads from wolf to Pekinese.

Looking at the dog through photography's history also reinforces and expands our notions of the compelling attachment between man and dog and the variety of ways it is expressed while giving us as well a picture of the vast array of canine types which science inexplicably has linked together.

These photographs, arranged chronologically, are assembled from public and private collections of fine art, and, while presenting a focus on the dog, also offer a view of the nature and the history of photography.

The dog has been a frequent subject in photography since its debut in 1839. The instant popularity of photography with a rising middle class, which wanted but could not afford painted portraits, coincided with the beginning of a heyday for the dog as household pet. In the newly leisured Victorian family, the dog was for the first time well fed, pampered, groomed, and shown and, as a member of the family, became an obvious candidate for the new portrait art. Daguerreotypes, the earliest photographic portrait process, required the subject to remain immobile for several minutes while the plate was registering the exposure and were therefore not compatible with frisky dogs. There are nevertheless some fine examples of daguerreotype pictures of more sedentary dogs—silvery and jewel-like miniatures, including some commissioned by Queen Victoria herself, who loved both dogs and photographs.

Simultaneous with the invention of the daguerreotype in France, William Henry Fox Talbot in England developed a negative/positive paper process. Most often used for scenic views, Talbot's 1844 calotype image of a dog grave marker is from *Sun Pictures in Scotland*, the first book ever illustrated with photographs.

By the 1850s, the small carte-de-visite image — made eight to twelve at a time on a single negative — became the favored medium of portrait photography, and was produced in the millions. Each little photograph cost only a few cents, and it was a popular custom to have the likeness of the dog made along with other family members. Meant to look proper and often posed on ornate chairs, every sort of mutt appears, distinguished by vivid quirks of personality. These charming studio poses were displayed with all the other family portraits (usually dour human beings) in the large, velvet-covered albums made especially for preserving them.

In an important technical step forward in photography, Eadweard Muybridge conducted systematic and successful experiments to stop action and capture movement beyond the capability of the unaided eye. He developed a complex system of shutters and tripping devices to prove that all four feet of a trotting horse were off the ground at one time. He was consequently invited to do extensive studies of humans and animals in motion. These serial studies featuring athletes, dancers, birds, buffaloes, and, yes, dogs formed a dictionary of animal locomotion for the use of artists. (Their viewing in rapid sequence led eventually to the birth of cinematography.)

After the introduction of the Kodak in 1887, much of the photographing of dogs became a family activity. There are exceptions, however, in the records made of show dogs by such skilled professionals as William Brown, and in a real affinity shown by a few photographers for dogs as subject matter.

The paramount example is Elliott Erwitt. One of the most successful of magazine photographers, whose work crosses boundaries between art and journalism, Erwitt has photographed hundreds of dogs throughout the world. His keen wit and observant eye present a picture of "canine persons" whose expressions of sadness, humor, and confusion often mirror our own. It is in these pictures, as in those of the numerous dogs on leashes photographed by Jean Pigozzi, another dog observer, that we wonder most about the essential nature of the dog. What traits of personality are really his and what has he acquired in the centuries with man? Would a wild dog smile as Erwitt's family dog appears to do?

Others, such as William Wegman, J.P. Hutto, and Antonio Mendoza engaged their dogs in collaborative efforts. Mendoza made an amusing dog's-eye-view series of his own dog, Leela, and that these photographs of ordinary dog behavior appear so funny says much about the way in which the spirit of the artist can suffuse his work and much about the way in which we invest the dog with human traits. J.P. Hutto's comic portraits of *Dogs Dressed as Men* point out, in the extreme, our tendencies to anthropomorphize. The figures of his Hawaiian Chow and Wall Street German Shepherd are so evenly divided between the characteristics of dog and the characteristics of man, they confuse the viewer.

William Wegman's ten-year collaboration with his Weimaraner, Man Ray, brought art-world celebrity status to both man and dog. The subject of a series of droll, often hilarious photographs, drawings, and videotapes, Man Ray, named for the famous Surrealist artist and photographer, apparently cooperated with his owner in a variety of silly schemes, as in the well-known 20-by-24-inch Polaroid portraits, where he appears in a variety of guises, such as a green frog, an outlandish pseudo-Polynesian, and as a bookend paired with a pink ceramic cat. A memorial portfolio of photographs was published when Man Ray, the dog, died in 1982.

For the most part, dogs have not been as popular a subject choice of photographers as, say, the landscape. The members of the Photo-Secession, the important turn-of-the-century movement that established photography as an art, made almost no images of dogs, and the master of the period, Edward Steichen, did not photograph either the wolfhounds that he raised (the picture of one of his dogs is by his wife) or his little three-legged dog, Tripod. Nevertheless almost every photographer of note has made at least one great photograph that, if not specifically of a dog, at least includes a dog.

Jacques-Henri Lartigue made many. From boyhood he was a practitioner of the new snapshot photography and included dogs in many of the charming photographs he took of his lively family (the photograph of Simone Roussel in 1904 was made when he was only ten). Lartigue's delightful pictures of family frolics and, later, the beautiful women of Paris preserve a romantic picture of France's Belle Epoque, when his engaging dogs romped through life with the same spirit as his friends and relatives.

André Kertész, too, looked at life with great affection. Making a personal record of the small details of daily life, first in Hungary where he was born and then in Paris (until he came to America in 1937), his photographs combine an originality and beauty of design with great sensitivity and warmth. In his classic photograph of *The Puppy,* as in many others, it appears he shared his good feelings with dogs as well as people.

August Sander, Berenice Abbott, Arnold Genthe, and Diane Arbus all excelled at portraiture. The Sander photographs represented here are from the extensive photographic survey of German social "types" that he produced in the 1920s (*Man of the Twentieth Century*). The dogs in Sander's images help to identify the character and status of the men with whom they stand. Similarly, the photographs by Genthe, Abbott, and Arbus, which are all representative examples of their work, illuminate an aspect of the human personality by portraying each subject in the role of owner-as-parent with his or her dog-as-child. It seems likely, as well, that sitters such as these would feel more comfortable sharing the focus of the camera's scrutinizing gaze with a favorite pet. Even Arbus's circus fat lady seems to feel that she herself is being less noticed by presenting her dog, Troubles, to the camera.

The dog-as-prop has a commercial role as well. Always a servant, the dog has traditionally been bred for his instincts to hunt, herd, and guard. In modern times, he has also been trained to lead the blind, perform circus stunts, sniff out contraband, try on contact lenses, and, in that ultimate of contemporary professions, work as an advertising model. In this latter role, the dog is valued less for

his obedience than for his spontaneity, his seemingly humorous behavior, and the infinite variety of styles in which he comes.
What makes Avedon's photograph of Veronica and Bruno so
arresting is surely not the scarf it is promoting; capturing the
viewer's attention is the true point here, and this the artist-animal
team does to perfection.

Near the end of the nineteenth century with the technical problems
of stopping action solved by faster lenses, shutters, and films, and
with the introduction of the small hand camera and roll film, ama-
teurs as well as artists took up photography. With great industry,
verve, and often wit, both kinds of photographers were active in a
short-lived postcard craze which struck Europe and America just
after 1900. Millions of photo cards produced an intimate view of
daily life, immortalizing small-town monuments, workers, family
groups, celebrations, and the weather with a certain equality of
treatment. The dog shows up with regularity in these informal,
homey pictures as the young boy's pal, the man's companion, the
family friend, and as comic character in hat or hairbow. Here it is
more evident than ever that the dog had become indivisible from
the ordinary household.

Photography cannot explain the social customs that allow one cul-
ture to devote itself to the dog as a pet while permitting another to
serve him as a stew; but it does show the diversity of these attitudes.
It is perhaps the photographer-journalist who gives us the best,
albeit unintended, look at the fortunes and fate of the modern dog.
Beginning with the appearance of the major picture magazines
(*Life, Look,* and others) in the 1930s, photo-journalists fanned out as

eyewitnesses to the world, composing in a straightforward manner photographs designed to provide information to the public. Interested, moreover, in reaching the most accessible emotions of the viewer to influence and shape opinion, their photographs usually portray the dog with sentimentality or with humor. Nevertheless, it is in this encompassing body of work that we see the multiplicity of arrangements made and relationships established between man and dog. Included here are the great war correspondent Robert Capa's touching photograph of the soldier with a puppy; social documentarian Margaret Bourke-White's graphic image of a boy and dog impoverished; and pictures by Robert Doisneau typical of his bemused glances at the daily life of France.

A new kind of photography developed in the 1970s and '80s. Oriented more toward art than journalism, photography turned inward, becoming a means of personal expression for the artist. With the use of decentralized composition, odd angles of vision, and distorted perspective and scale, the work often reflects a prevailing view of a world now out of kilter. Lee Friedlander's urban dog as the only sign of life on a deserted city street and Mark Cohen's shepherd seen from the rear serve as metaphors of modern isolation. Cohen's people too, torsos only, underline this point. In an ironic return to the dog as portrait-subject, Tod Papageorge's photograph of photographers at work comments on the strange priorities of modern life. Helen Levitt, one of the first of the contemporary "street photographers" (who began her career in the 1940s), reveals a gentler view of urban life; her photographs, most frequently of city children, are often about settling for the simple

pleasures and the riskiness of having too much hope. Nicholas
Nixon also concentrates on people, but often notices and includes
their dogs. He searches for small signs of warmth enduring in the
human spirit and often finds them in gestures of affection between
man and dog.

This book records moments when photographer and dog have met
—and brings together pedigrees and mutts, their beauty equal in
the artist's eye—in pictures expressing the tribute of Elizabeth
Barrett Browning:

> Therefore to this dog will I,
> Tenderly not scornfully,
> Render praise and favor.

R.S.
1984

The Dog Observed

William Henry Fox Talbot, from *Sun Pictures in Scotland,* 1844
CALOTYPE

Anonymous American, 1858

AMBROTYPE

Anonymous American, c. 1855

DAGUERREOTYPE

Anonymous American, c. 1862

AMBROTYPE

Anonymous American, c. 1848
DAGUERREOTYPE

Anonymous American, c. 1850-52
DAGUERREOTYPE

André Adolfe-Eugène Disdéri, *Digo Djanetto*, France, 1854
ALBUMEN PRINT

Bisson *frères*, Study of a dog, France, 1850s
ALBUMEN PRINT

Alinari, *Cane di Terranuova*, Florence, c. 1850

ALBUMEN PRINT

Anonymous American, c. 1868

TINTYPE

Oscar Gustave Rejlander, *A Secret,* England, c. 1860
ALBUMEN PRINT

Lavalle, Paris, Carte-de-visite, c. 1872
ALBUMEN PRINT

O. LAWSON,
PORTRAIT PAINTER,
High Street, Tunbridge Wells.

Various photographers, Cartes-de-visite, c. 1860s
ALBUMEN PRINTS

Peter Henry Emerson, *The Poacher — A Hare in View,* from *Pictures of East Anglian Life,* London, 1888

PHOTOGRAVURE

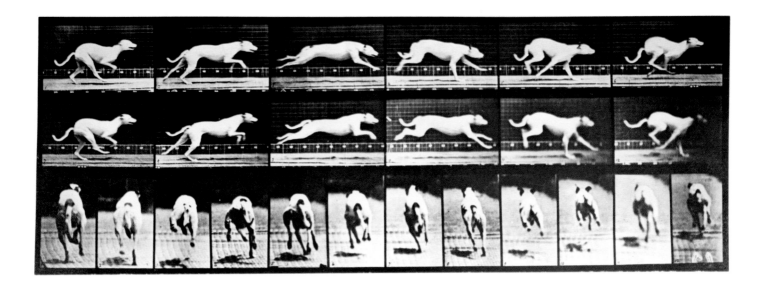

Eadweard Muybridge, *"Maggie" galloping,* from *Animal Locomotion,* Philadelphia, 1887

CALOTYPE

Lawton S. Gray Parker, *Billy Green and Foolish*, 1890

Paul Nadar, *Le Chien de Monsieur Pierson*, France, 1890s

Arnold Genthe, *Mrs. Patrick Campbell,* 1902

Camille Puyo, France, c. 1900

Darius Kinsey, *On the Spring Boards and in the Undercut* (Washington bolt cutter and daughters), 1905

Jacques-Henri Lartigue, *My cousin, Simone Roussel*, 1904

Jacques-Henri Lartigue, *Avenue du Bois de Boulogne*, Paris, 1911

Anonymous American, 1910, Postcard

Anonymous American, c. 1912, Postcard

Anonymous American, c. 1912, Postcard

Anonymous American, c. 1910, Postcard

Anonymous American, c. 1912, Postcard

Anonymous American, 1938?, Postcard

Jacques-Henri Lartigue, *Tupy and M. Plitt,* 1912

Anonymous American, *Marksbury Myra*, c. 1915, Postcard

Brown Bros., *Crossing Great Slave Lake in Winter,* c. 1911

Robert Flaherty, *The Huskie,* from the Revillon Frères portfolio, 1923
PHOTOGRAVURE

Edward S. Curtis, *Assiniboin Hunter,* 1926

PHOTOGRAVURE

August Sander, *Notary,* Cologne, 1924

August Sander, *Village Schoolteacher*, Westerwald, 1921

André Kertész, *The Puppy*, 1926

André Kertész, *The Concierge's Dog*, 1926

Berenice Abbott, *Mme. Guerin*, Paris, c. 1926

D'Ora, *Dora Duby,* Paris, c. 1927

André Kertész, *The Luxembourg Garden in the Afternoon*, 1928

Martin Munkacsi, *Dog and Hand,* Berlin, c. 1929

Lotte Jacobi, *Lil Dagover*, Berlin, 1930

T. Lux Feininger, *Man in Mask with Dog,* late 1920s
"The Bauhaus dog: Arras. Man: Clemens Roseler. Mask: Lux Feininger"

Dana Steichen, *Edward Steichen with Fingal of Ambleside*, c. 1930

Brassaï (Gyula Halász), *Kiki avec ses amies — Thérèse Treize de Cara et Lily,* c. 1932

Dr. Erich Salomon, *Dog on Train between Chicago and New York,* 1932

Margaret Bourke-White, *Sharecropper's Home,* 1937

Lisette Model, *Promenade des Anglais*, Nice, 1937

Lisette Model, *Promenade des Anglais,* Nice, 1937

Weegee (Arthur Fellig), *New York*, c. 1940

James Van Der Zee, *Rover and I*, c. 1940

Horst, *Gertrude Stein and Basket*, Paris, 1946

William Brown, *R. E. Allen's English Springer Spaniel, Champion Timpanago's Melinda with H. Sangster,*
Best — Sporting Group, Westminster Kennel Club Dog Show, February 1942

Louise Rosskam, *Cody, Wyoming,* July 1944

Georgi Lipskerov, *Russian Soldiers in Berlin,* c. 1945

Helen Levitt, *New York,* c. 1942

Dan Weiner, *East End Avenue*, New York, 1950

Anonymous, *Training Police Dogs*, Sydney, New South Wales, Australia, c. 1948

Richard Avedon, *Veronica Compton and Bruno,* scarf by John Frederics, New York studio, July 1949

Robert Doisneau, *Wanda Wiggles Her Hips*, France, 1953

Robert Capa, *French soldier and dog,* Indochina, May 1954

Elliott Erwitt, *Wyoming,* 1953

Sid Avery, *Humphrey Bogart, Lauren Bacall, son Steven with dogs Harvey, George, and Baby,*
from *The Saturday Evening Post,* 1952

Ilse Bing, *Three Schnauzers and Three Shadows*, 1955

Toni Frissell, *Hounds on the Scent*, Meath Hunt, Ireland, November 1956

John Szarkowski, *Mathew Brady in the Backyard* (Ashland, Wisconsin), 1953

Emmet Gowin, *Danville, Virginia,* 1969

Elliott Erwitt, *Brussels,* 1957

Mario Giacomelli, *Zingari,* 1959

Nina Leen, *Whippet*, New York, 1964
(Champion Courtenay Fleetfoot of Pennyworth, Best of Show — Westminster Kennel Club Dog Show)
From a color photograph

Manuel Carrillo, *Mexico,* 1960s

Elliott Erwitt, *USA*, 1964

Manuel Alvarez Bravo, *Dreams Ought to Be Believed*, Mexico, 1966

Diane Arbus, *Circus Fat Lady and Her Dog, Troubles,* 1964

Henri Cartier-Bresson, *Outside a Bistro*, 1968/69

Daido Moriyama, *Stray Dog*, Misawa, Japan, 1971

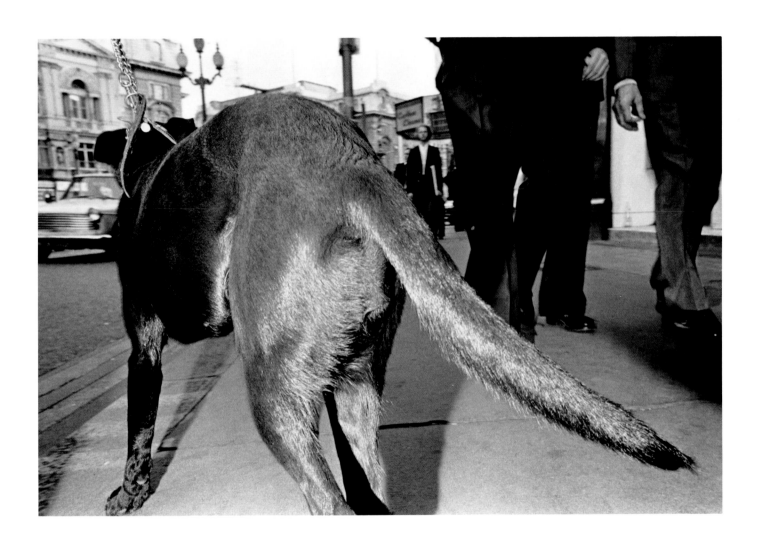

Mark Cohen, *London*, 1975

Helen Levitt, *New York,* 1972
From a dye-transfer print

Lee Friedlander, *Los Angeles*, 1965

Lee Friedlander, *Albuquerque, New Mexico*, 1972

Harry Callahan, *Horseneck Beach,* 1974

Elliott Erwitt, *New York,* 1974

Garry Winogrand, *New York,* c. 1975

Sylvia Plachy, *Budapest, Hungary,* 1976

Harvey Stein, *Black and White Dog,* 1972

Robert Doisneau, *Dog on Wheels*, Paris, 1977

Jacques-Henri Lartigue, *Brittany,* 1976

William Wegman, *Man Ray Contemplating the Bust of Man Ray,* 1978

William Wegman, *Dusted*, 1982
From a Polaroid 20″ x 24″ color photograph

William Wegman, *Bookends*, 1981
From a Polaroid 20″ x 24″ color photograph

Antonio Mendoza, *Untitled,* from the Leela Series, 1979

Antonio Mendoza, *Untitled,* from the Leela Series, 1979

Antonio Mendoza, *Untitled,* from the Leela Series, 1979

Nicholas Nixon, *MDC Park, Allston, Massachusetts,* 1979

Jean Pigozzi, *New York,* 1979

Jean Pigozzi, *New York,* 1973

Nicholas Nixon, *Shiloh, Tennessee,* 1978

Nicholas Nixon, *Harlan, Kentucky,* 1982

Marvin Gasoi, *Venice, California*, 1982
From a color transparency

J. P. Hutto, *Dogs Dressed as Men*, 1981/82

J. P. Hutto, *Dogs Dressed as Men*, 1981/82

Horst, *Andy Warhol's Studio*, New York, 1983
From a color transparency

Robert Mapplethorpe, *Dovanna and Albert*, New York, 1983

Robert Mapplethorpe, *Rory, Owned by Steven Aronson*, New York, 1983

Tod Papageorge, *New York*, 1980

Photographic Credits

page 136 Courtesy the photographer and Holly Solomon Gallery, New York;
Collection Gifford Myers, Pasadena

137 Courtesy the photographer, Holly Solomon Gallery, New York,
and Walker Art Center, Minneapolis; Collection Martin Z. Margolies

139 Courtesy the photographer

140 Courtesy the photographer

141 Courtesy the photographer

143 Courtesy Daniel Wolf, Inc., New York, and Pace/MacGill Gallery, New York

144 Courtesy the photographer

145 Courtesy the photographer

146 Courtesy Daniel Wolf, Inc., New York, and Pace/MacGill Gallery, New York

147 Courtesy Daniel Wolf, Inc., New York, and Pace/MacGill Gallery, New York

149 Courtesy the photographer

150 Courtesy the photographer

151 Courtesy the photographer

153 Courtesy the photographer and *Glamour;* © 1983 The Condé Nast Publications, Inc.

155 Courtesy the photographer and The Agency Models, New York

157 Courtesy the photographer

159 Courtesy the photographer and Daniel Wolf, Inc., New York

A Note on the Type

The text of this book was set in film in Cochin, a
type face named for Charles Nicolas Cochin the
younger, an eighteenth-century French engraver.
It is patterned after the copperplate lettering used
to caption the engravings of the period. Cochin,
unlike many of his contemporaries, was as much
an engraver as a designer, and deeply interested in
the technique of the art.

All original photographs are gelatin silver prints
unless otherwise indicated.

Copy photography by Scott Hyde

Composed by Characters, New York, New York
Printed by The Rembrandt Press, Milford, Conn.
Bound by The Book Press, Brattleboro, Vermont
Designed by Judith Henry and Iris Weinstein